GREAT MINDS® WIT & WISDOM

Grade K Module 1:
The Five Senses

Student Edition

COPYRIGHT STATEMENT

Published by Great Minds®.

Copyright ©2016 Great Minds®. All rights reserved. No part of this work may be reproduced or used in any form or by any means—graphic, electronic, or mechanical, including photocopying or information storage and retrieval systems—without written permission from the copyright holder.

ISBN: 978-1-68386-017-4

Table of Contents

Handout 1A: Question Corner Signs

Handout 4A: Sensory Cards

Handout 5A: First Page of Sensory Book

Handout 10A: Book Cover

Handout 13A: Sight and Hearing Cards

Handout 14A: Drawing of City Street

Handout 15A: Complete Sentences

Handout 16A: Book Cover

Handout 18A: *Flower Day*

Handout 23A: Sketch of Page 3 in *Rap a Tap Tap*

Handout 24A: Sketch of Page 18 in *Rap a Tap Tap*

Handout 26A: Rhyming Cards

Handout 26B: Preposition Cards

Handout 28A: Bojangles and Prepositions

Handout 29A: Have Conversations Response Cards

Volume of Reading Reflection

Wit & Wisdom Parent Tip Sheet

Name:

Handout 1A: Question Corner Signs

Directions: Create questions about the text using the question word on the sign.

WHO?

Name: _____

WHAT?

Name: _____

WHEN?

Name: _____

WHERE?

Name: _____

WHY?

Name: _____

HOW?

Name:

Handout 4A: Sensory Cards

Directions: Identify the sense on the card and explain how you used this sense to a peer.

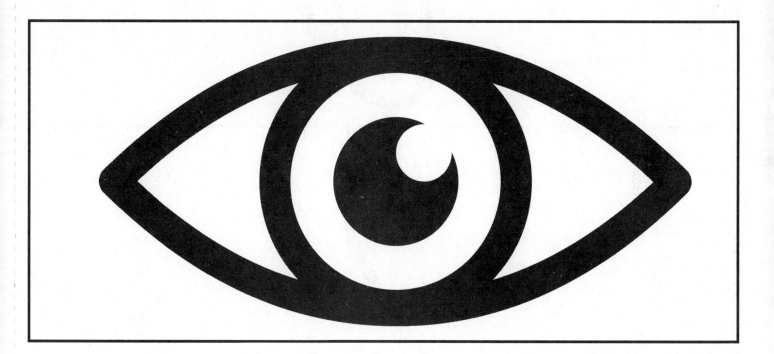

Name: _____

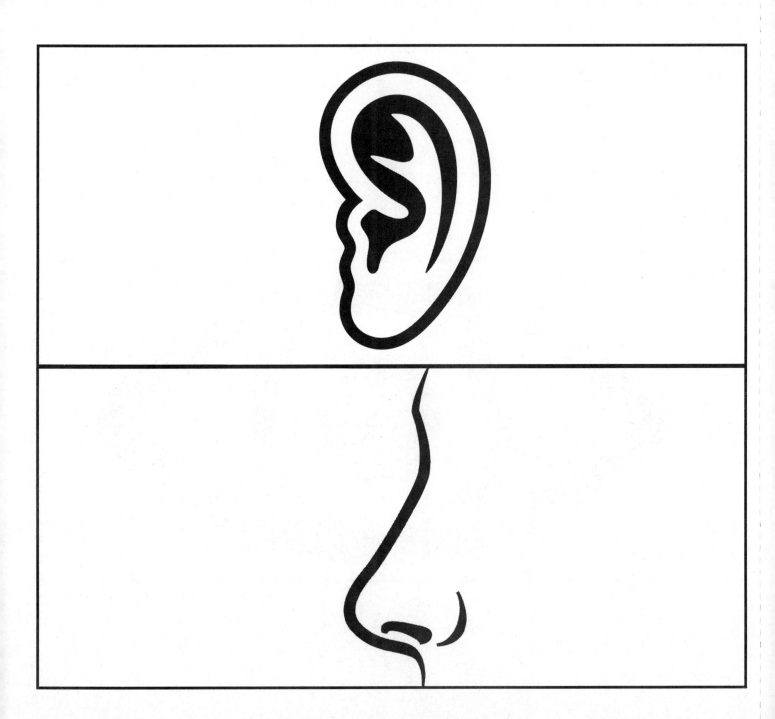

Name:

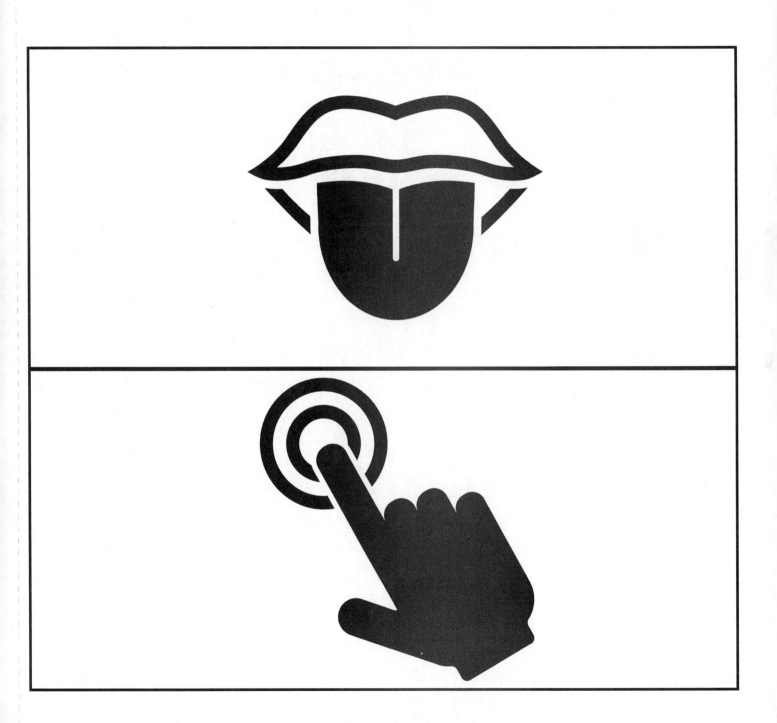

Name: _____

Handout 5A: First Page of Sensory Book

Directions: Cut out this page and attach it as the first page of the group Sensory Book.

Our senses help us enjoy the world.

Name: _____

Handout 10A: Book Cover

Directions: Cut out this page and attach it as the cover of the Sensory Book. Create a drawing for the cover in the large box below.

The boy  uses his senses to learn about the world.

Handout 13A: Sight and Hearing Cards

Directions: Hold up one card to signal what sense CJ is using in the text. Cite examples from the text.

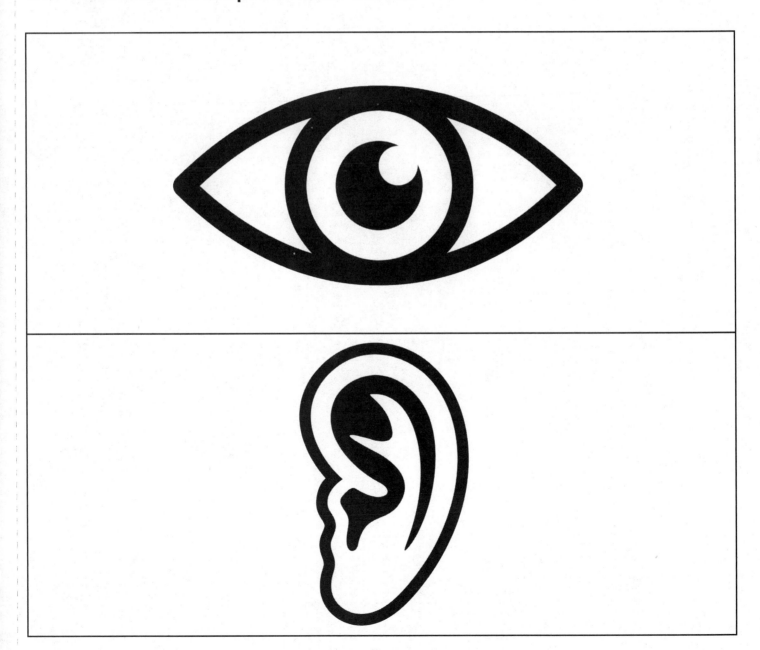

Handout 14A: Drawing of City Street

Directions: Add text details to the drawing based on the words and illustrations in the text.

Name:

Handout 15A: Complete Sentences

Directions: Verbally create a complete sentence using each image as the "who" in the sentence.

Name: _____

Handout 16A: Book Cover

Directions: Cut out this page and attach it as the book cover. Create a drawing for the cover in the large box below.

CJ  uses his senses to learn about the world.

Name: _____

Handout 18A: *Flower Day*

Directions: Use letters to label the people and things in the picture.

Copyright © 2016 Great Minds®

Name: _____

Handout 23A: Sketch of Page 3 in *Rap a Tap Tap*

Directions: Use letters to label the people and things in the picture.

Name:

Handout 24A: Sketch of Page 18 in *Rap a Tap Tap*

Directions: Write at least two labels for the illustration.

Name: _____

Handout 26A: Rhyming Cards (Page 1 of 5)

Directions: Signal when you hear a word that rhymes with the word on the card. Identify the rhyming words.

GREET

Name: _____

Handout 26A: Rhyming Cards (Page 2 of 5)

Directions: Signal when you hear a word that rhymes with the word on the card. Identify the rhyming words.

Name:

Handout 26A: Rhyming Cards (Page 3 of 5)

Directions: Signal when you hear a word that rhymes with the word on the card. Identify the rhyming words.

SKIDS

Name:

Handout 26A: Rhyming Cards (Page 4 of 5)

Directions: Signal when you hear a word that rhymes with the word on the card. Identify the rhyming words.

Name:

Handout 26A: Rhyming Cards (Page 5 of 5)

Directions: Signal when you hear a word that rhymes with the word on the card. Identify the rhyming words.

Handout 26B: Preposition Cards (Page 1 of 2)

Directions: Use the preposition on the card to complete a sentence frame.

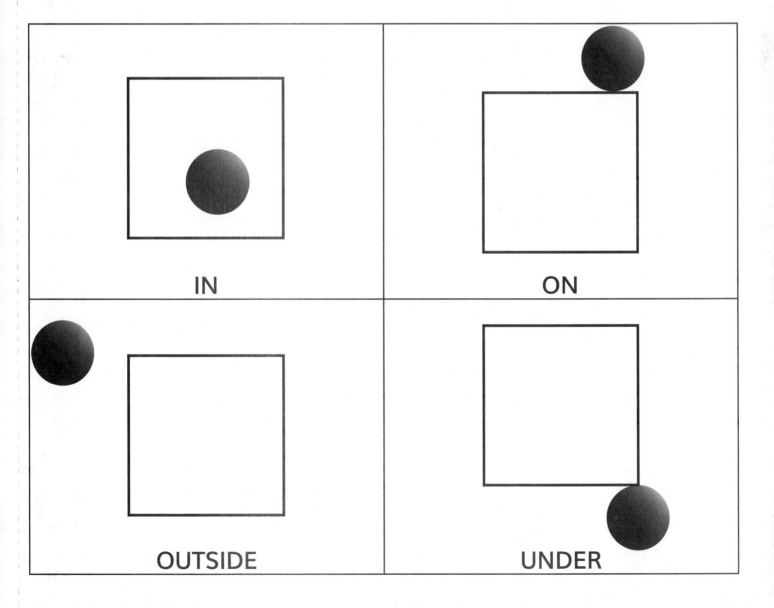

Name:

Handout 26B: Preposition Cards (Page 2 of 2)

Name:

Handout 28A: Bojangles and Prepositions

Directions: Create complete sentences with prepositions by moving the image of Bojangles.

Name: _____

Handout 29A: Have Conversations Response Cards

Directions: Use this card to ask a peer a question about their text evidence as you have conversations.

What text evidence did you use?	What text evidence did you use?
What text evidence did you use?	What text evidence did you use?
What text evidence did you use?	What text evidence did you use?

Volume of Reading Reflection

The Five Senses, Kindergarten, Module 1

Student Name: _____

Text: _____

Author: _____

Topic: _____

Genre/Type of Book: _____

Share what you know about the five senses by answering one question in each category (Wonder, Organize, Reveal, Distill, Know) below. Draw a picture or tell your teacher your answer to each question.

1. Wonder: What does the front cover tell us about the book? What does the back cover tell us about the book? What do you see on the front or back cover that gives clues about what happens in the text?

2. Wonder: Why did you choose to read this book about the five senses? What did you notice about the book that made you want to read it? Point to the details that you noticed.

3. Wonder: What are you wondering about the five senses after reading this book?

4. Organize: How does this book teach that you have five senses? What key details did you notice in the illustrations? Point to the key details that you noticed.

5. Organize: What did you learn about how our senses work from this book? Draw a picture showing what you learned.

6. Organize: Complete the following sentence by drawing the sense (smell, touch, taste, sight, hearing) in the first blank and what you used to learn about it (eyes, ears, nose, hands, tongue) in the second blank:

   In this book, I learned about my sense of _____ with my _____.

7. Reveal: Find an important idea about one of your senses in the book. Draw the important detail that you noticed on the page. Tell your teacher why that page is important.

8. Reveal: What is one important way the author shows or uses the five senses in the book? Point to an example in the book.

9. Reveal: How does a character use his or her senses to learn about the world around them? Explain what you heard in the text and point to the illustration that shows the character using his or her senses.

10. Reveal: Choose one of the illustrations or drawings that helped you better understand how our senses help us. Share with your teacher how this illustration helped you.

11. Distill: Before reading the book, what did you know about the five senses? Give an example of an idea that you knew that was also explained in the book.

12. Distill: What new information do you now know about the five senses? Share the new idea that you learned.

13. Know: How do people use their senses to learn about the world?

14. Know: Should other kids who are interested in learning about the five senses read this book? Was it helpful or interesting to you? Why or why not?

WIT & WISDOM PARENT TIP SHEET

WHAT IS MY KINDERGARTEN STUDENT LEARNING IN MODULE 1?

Wit & Wisdom is our English curriculum. It builds knowledge of key topics in history, science, and literature through the study of excellent texts. By reading and responding to stories and nonfiction texts, we will build knowledge of the following topics:

Module 1: The Five Senses

Module 2: Once Upon a Farm

Module 3: America Then and Now

Module 4: The Continents

In this first module, we will study the five senses. Studying the five senses lays a foundation for knowledge of human biology. We will learn how we see, hear, taste, touch, and smell as we ask the question: *How do our senses help us to learn?*

OUR CLASS WILL READ THESE BOOKS:

Picture Books (Informational)

- *My Five Senses*, Aliki
- *My Five Senses*, Margaret Miller
- *Rap a Tap Tap*, Leo and Diane Dillon

Picture Books (Literary)

- *Chicka Chicka Boom Boom*, Bill Martin Jr. and John Archambault; illustrations, Lois Ehlert
- *Last Stop on Market Street*, Matt de la Pena; illustrations, Christian Robinson

Articles

- "Great Depression," Children's Encyclopedia
- "The Harlem Renaissance," Brian Brown

OUR CLASS WILL WATCH THESE VIDEOS:

- "Bojangles Step Dance"
- "Chicka Chicka Boom Boom"
- "Eight-Year-Old Tap Prodigy Little Luke"

OUR CLASS WILL EXAMINE THESE PAINTINGS:

- *Flower Day*, Diego Rivera
- *Le Gourmet*, Pablo Picasso

OUR CLASS WILL ASK THESE QUESTIONS:

- What are our five senses?
- How do people use their senses to learn about the world?
- How does CJ use his senses to learn about the world in *Last Stop on Market Street*?
- How do our senses help us learn from *Chicka Chicka Boom Boom*?
- How do our senses help us learn from *Rap a Tap Tap*?
- How do our senses help us learn?

QUESTIONS TO ASK AT HOME:

As you read with your Kindergarten student, ask:

- *What do you notice and wonder?*

BOOKS TO READ AT HOME:

- *Geraldine, the Music Mouse*, Leo Lionni
- *Brown Bear, Brown Bear, What Do You See?* Bill Martin Jr.
- *Polar Bear, Polar Bear, What Do You Hear?* Bill Martin Jr.
- *The Listening Walk*, Paul Showers
- *Drum Dream Girl*, Margarita Engle
- *Hello Ocean*, Pam Muñoz Ryan
- *Rain*, Manya Stojic
- *Owl Moon*, Jane Yolen
- *Snowy Day*, Ezra Jack Keats

- *Little Fur Family*, Margaret Wise Brown
- *Every Second Something Happens: Poems for the Mind and the Senses*, Christine San José
- *Ada Twist, Scientist*, Andrea Beaty
- *No One Saw*, Bob Raczka

PLACES YOU CAN VISIT TO TALK ABOUT THE FIVE SENSES:

Visit an art museum or art exhibit together. Take time to look at the art and ask:

- What are you wondering about the five senses after looking at this art?
- What do you notice?
- What's happening in this work of art?
- How do people use their senses to learn about the world?

CREDITS

Great Minds® has made every effort to obtain permission for the reprinting of all copyrighted material. If any owner of copyrighted material is not acknowledged herein, please contact Great Minds® for proper acknowledgment in all future editions and reprints of this module.

- All material from the *Common Core State Standards for English Language Arts & Literacy in History/Social Studies, Science, and Technical Subjects* © Copyright 2010 National Governors Association Center for Best Practices and Council of Chief State School Officers. All rights reserved.
- All images are used under license from Shutterstock.com unless otherwise noted.
- For updated credit information, please visit **http://witeng.link/credits**.

ACKNOWLEDGMENTS

Great Minds® Staff

The following writers, editors, reviewers, and support staff contributed to the development of this curriculum.

Ann Brigham, Lauren Chapalee, Sara Clarke, Emily Climer, Lorraine Griffith, Emily Gula, Sarah Henchey, Trish Huerster, Stephanie Kane-Mainier, Lior Klirs, Liz Manolis, Andrea Minich, Lynne Munson, Marya Myers, Rachel Rooney, Aaron Schifrin, Danielle Shylit, Rachel Stack, Sarah Turnage, Michelle Warner, Amy Wierzbicki, Margaret Wilson, and Sarah Woodard.

Colleagues and Contributors

We are grateful for the many educators, writers, and subject-matter experts who made this program possible.

David Abel, Robin Agurkis, Elizabeth Bailey, Julianne Barto, Amy Benjamin, Andrew Biemiller, Charlotte Boucher, Sheila Byrd-Carmichael, Jessica Carloni, Eric Carey, Janine Cody, Rebecca Cohen, Elaine Collins, Tequila Cornelious, Beverly Davis, Matt Davis, Thomas Easterling, Jeanette Edelstein, Kristy Ellis, Moira Clarkin Evans, Charles Fischer, Marty Gephart, Kath Gibbs, Natalie Goldstein, Christina Gonzalez, Mamie Goodson, Nora Graham, Lindsay Griffith, Brenna Haffner, Joanna Hawkins, Elizabeth Haydel, Steve Hettleman, Cara Hoppe, Ashley Hymel, Carol Jago, Jennifer Johnson, Mason Judy, Gail Kearns, Shelly Knupp, Sarah Kushner, Shannon Last, Suzanne Lauchaire, Diana Leddy, David Liben, Farren Liben, Jennifer Marin, Susannah Maynard, Cathy McGath, Emily McKean, Jane Miller, Rebecca Moore, Cathy Newton, Turi Nilsson, Julie Norris, Galemarie Ola, Michelle Palmieri, Meredith Phillips, Shilpa Raman, Tonya Romayne, Emmet Rosenfeld, Jennifer Ruppel, Mike Russoniello, Deborah Samley, Casey Schultz, Renee Simpson, Rebecca Sklepovich, Amelia Swabb, Kim Taylor, Vicki Taylor, Melissa Thomson, Lindsay Tomlinson, Melissa Vail, Keenan Walsh, Julia Wasson, Lynn Welch, Yvonne Guerrero Welch, Emily Whyte, Lynn Woods, and Rachel Zindler.

Early Adopters

The following early adopters provided invaluable insight and guidance for Wit & Wisdom:

- Bourbonnais School District 53 • Bourbonnais, IL
- Coney Island Prep Middle School • Brooklyn, NY
- Gate City Charter School for the Arts • Merrimack, NH
- Hebrew Academy for Special Children • Brooklyn, NY
- Paris Independent Schools • Paris, KY
- Saydel Community School District • Saydel, IA
- Strive Collegiate Academy • Nashville, TN
- Valiente College Preparatory Charter School • South Gate, CA
- Voyageur Academy • Detroit, MI

Design Direction provided by Alton Creative, Inc.

Project management support, production design, and copyediting services provided by ScribeConcepts.com

Copyediting services provided by Fine Lines Editing

Product management support provided by Sandhill Consulting